Math in Focus®
Singapore Math
by Marshall Cavendish

Implementation Guide

Support for Planning and Instruction

COMMON CORE

Copyright © by Houghton Mifflin Harcourt Publishing Company

All rights reserved. No part of this work may be reproduced or transmitted in any form or by any means, electronic or mechanical, including photocopying or recording, or by any information storage and retrieval system, without the prior written permission of the copyright owner unless such copying is expressly permitted by federal copyright law. Requests for permission to make copies of any part of the work should be addressed to Houghton Mifflin Harcourt Publishing Company, Attn: Contracts, Copyrights, and Licensing, 9400 South Park Center Loop, Orlando, Florida 32819.

Printed in the U.S.A.

ISBN 978-0-547-81641-8

10 11 12 13 14 15 1689 20 19 18 17 16 15 14
4500486551   A B C D E F G

If you have received these materials as examination copies free of charge, Houghton Mifflin Harcourt Publishing Company retains title to the materials and they may not be resold. Resale of examination copies is strictly prohibited.

Possession of this publication in print format does not entitle users to convert this publication, or any portion of it, into electronic format.

Contents

What is *Math in Focus* and Singapore Math?

Welcome to *Math in Focus™: Singapore Math* by Marshall Cavendish. This guide is intended to help you get started implementing *Math in Focus* in your classroom. As you work through the guide, you'll develop an understanding of the resources available to you in the *Math in Focus* program.

Math In Focus is the United States edition of the most widely used curriculum in Singapore, which has consistently been the top-performing country in international assessments such as TIMSS and PISA. Because Singapore has been so consistently successful in math, its curriculum was one of the main models used to write the Common Core State Standards. Singapore Math helped to shape not only the content of the Common Core State Standards but also especially the philosophy and pedagogy.

Before we get started, we want you to understand the underlying premise of Singapore Math that is represented in this pentagon. This is the Mathematics Framework from the Ministry of Education in Singapore.

- Problem solving is at the heart of any math program—you learn math to solve problems.

- You must possess the conceptual base to understand and solve problems.

- You must possess the relevant skills and understand the processes involved in problem solving.

- You must possess metacognition—the understanding of your learning processes.

- Finally, you must possess confidence and persistence to be a successful problem solver.

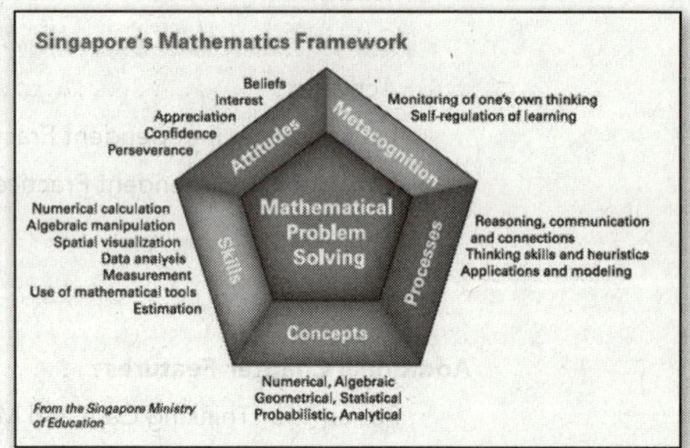

Math in Focus Components for Grades 1–5:

- **Teacher's Edition A and B.**

- **Student Book A and B** are hard cover, non-consumable books that students use every day. Book A focuses primarily on number and operation, while the primary focus of Book B is geometry and measurement.

- **Workbooks A and B** are consumable books that provide independent practice both in school and at home. The work is assigned when students demonstrate they can do the problems independently.

- **Reteach A and B, Extra Practice A and B, and Enrichment A and B** provide material for differentiation. The books come as Blackline masters, and the material is also available online.

- **Assessments** are available both as Blackline masters and online. They include a pre-test and chapter test for each chapter as well as cumulative, semester, and year-end assessments. There are two versions for the chapter tests: one in the Student Book or Workbook and one in the Assessments book.

- **School-to-Home Connections** provides a newsletter for each chapter to be sent home to facilitate communication with families. They contain "at home" activities that align with the chapters in *Math in Focus*.

- **Manipulative Kits** are an integral part of *Math in Focus*. You may have a new manipulative kit, or you may be using previously purchased interlocking cubes and base-ten materials.

- **Virtual Manipulatives** are also an integral part of *Math in Focus*. Virtual manipulatives are available online.

- **Achieving Facts Fluency** offers activities and worksheets to build computational fluency.

Getting Started

Teacher Tip:

Use sticky notes, tabs, and if allowed, a highlighter to take notes right in your Teacher's Edition. You may want to find all the planning pieces listed here before you go further in this guide.

How to Plan a Chapter and a Lesson

One benefit of the *Math in Focus* curriculum is that while it includes many different activities and instructional practices, the structure of each grade level and each chapter is the same. Once you learn this structure, you will find it quite easy to plan your lessons.

As you plan to teach each chapter and its lessons, we suggest you work through the parts of each chapter and lesson in the following order:

- Scope and Sequence
- Chapter Overview
- Chapter Wrap Up
- Chapter Review/Test
- Chapter Planning Guide
- Chapter Introduction
- Recall Prior Knowledge and Quick Check
- Transition Guide and Transition Planner
- Lesson Planning
  - Teach/Learn
  - Guided Practice
  - Reteach
  - Enrichment
- Put on Your Thinking Cap! and Math Journal
- Assessment

Refer to your Teacher's Edition as we work through each of these elements.

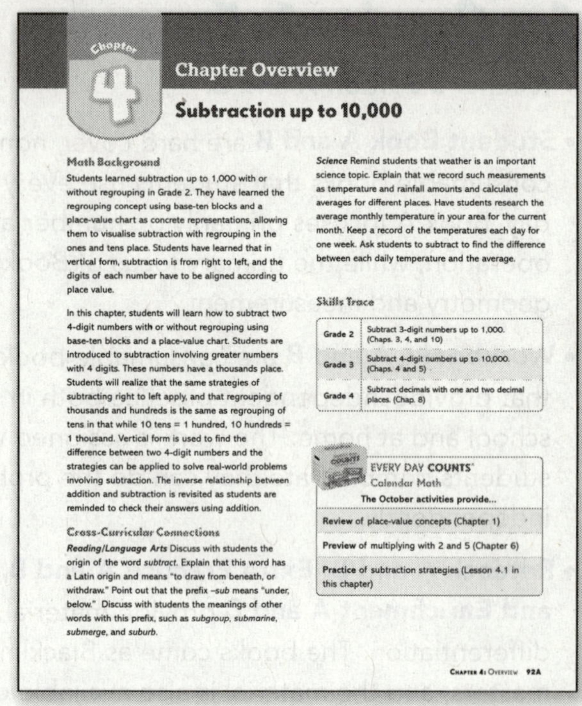

Grade 3 is shown as an example.

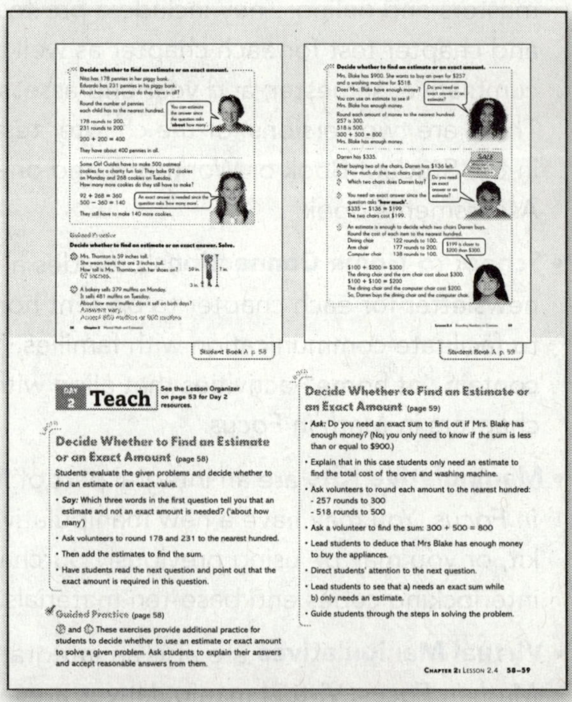

Grade 3 is shown as an example.

Chapter Planning

Teacher Tip:

Look at the Table of Contents in Teacher's Edition Book B because it lists the contents of both books.

Scope and Sequence

Before you begin planning the first chapter, you will probably want to know the sequence of topics you will be teaching this year, especially because it may differ from sequences you've used previously. In particular, as you look at the Table of Contents for Book A and Book B, you will see that many arithmetic topics are taught early in the school year and that these are followed with geometry and measurement topics. The Table of Contents in Book A lists only the chapters from Book A. You may find it more helpful to look at the Table of Contents for Book B, since it contains chapters from both Book A and Book B.

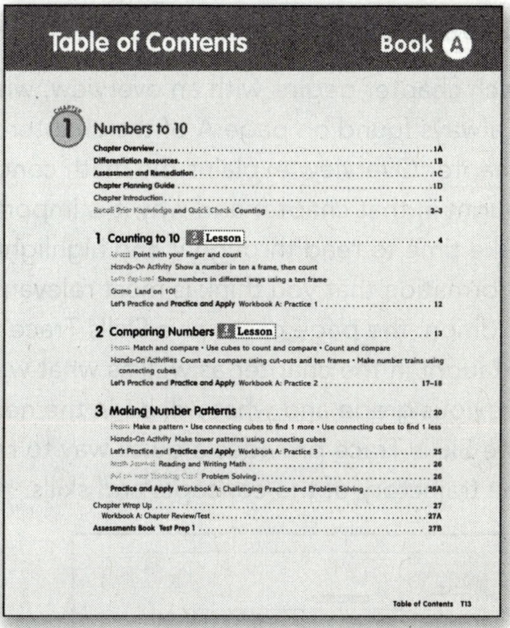

After reviewing the Table of Contents, turn to the Scope and Sequence table in Teacher's Edition A. On these pages you'll see the scope of the topics in your grade as well as what has been taught in the previous grade and what will be taught in the next grade. Of course you will want to look in particular at the content of the chapter you are teaching, but these pages will also give you a general idea of all the content you will be teaching this year. For example, the first chapter in Grade 3 is on numbers to ten thousand. Students will read, write, compare, and look for patterns to 10,000. The first chapter for Grade 2 covers the same ideas but with numbers only to 1000. Fourth graders will extend their understanding to larger numbers.

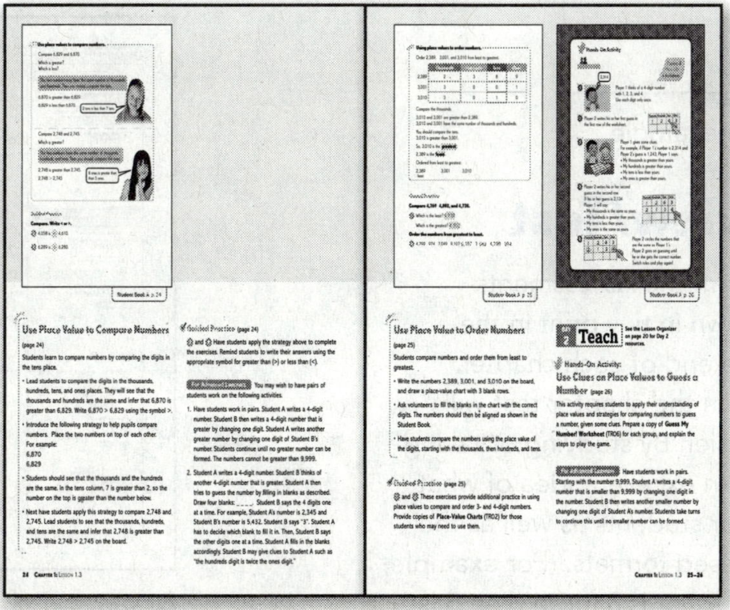

Grade 3 is shown as an example.

Chapter Overview

Each chapter begins with an overview, which is always found on page A of the chapter. The Chapter Overview explains the math concept taught in that chapter and why it is important. Take time to read through it and highlight any information that you think is most relevant. In addition, the page contains a Skills Trace for what is taught in the chapter as well as what was in the previous grade and what will be in the next grade. The Skills Trace provides a quick way to recognize the trajectory of the concepts and skills.

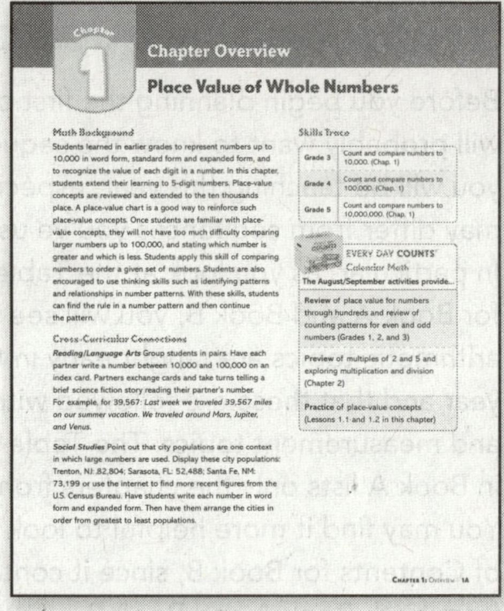

Grade 4 is shown as an example.

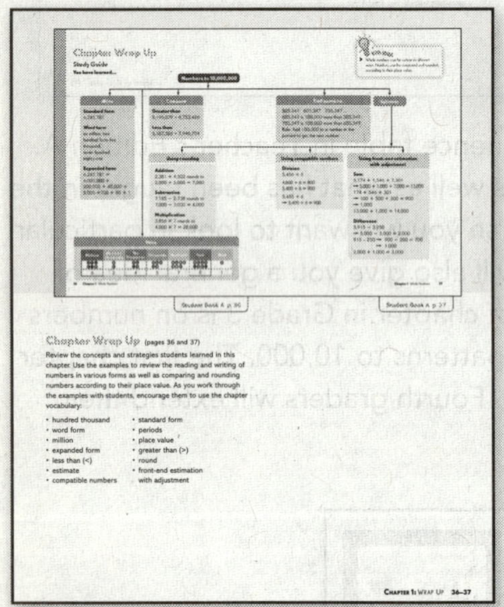

Grade 5 is shown as an example.

Chapter Wrap Up

The Chapter Wrap Up appears on the last page of every chapter, just before the Chapter Review/Test. It can also be found in the Student Book. The visual organizer in the Chapter Wrap Up provides an easy way to see what is taught in the chapter and the order it is presented in.

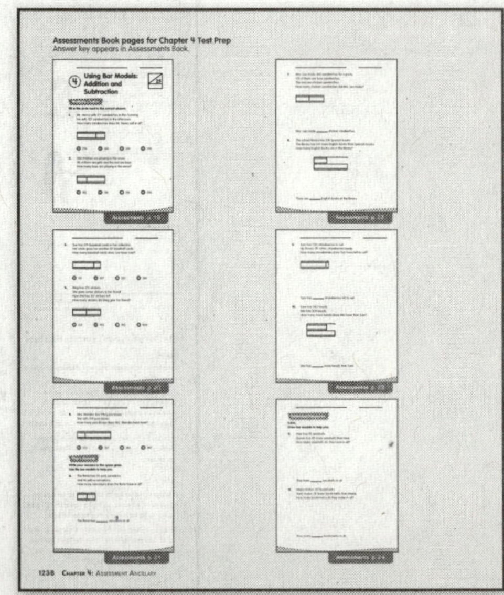

Grade 2 is shown as an example.

Chapter Review/Test

Use the chapter test from the Assessments book, which is also shown in tiny print in the Teacher's Edition at the end of each chapter. Working backwards from the chapter test will make your planning easier. By studying or taking the test, you will have an excellent idea of what will be expected of your students as well as the complexity of the assessed formats. (For example, for first graders, asking what is 3 more than 5 is more complex than asking what is 5 + 3.)

Chapter Planning Guide

The Chapter Planning Guide, which begins on page D of each chapter, is the best place to see how the chapter is laid out into lessons. Notice that some lessons require only one day, while others need two or three days. In the Chapter Planning Guide, you will see the teaching sequence of concepts, the length of time ideally expected, the objectives and vocabulary for each lesson, the printed materials available to you to teach the lesson, the necessary manipulatives, and the connection to the Common Core State Standards.

Take special note of two features as you look at these pages. First, notice all the lessons in a chapter focus on one big idea or concept. The chapter does not jump around or include extraneous material. This is one of the noted features of Singapore Math. Next notice how carefully the lessons are sequenced. Each lesson logically flows from the previous one. Students first develop an understanding of the concept, then develop more efficient and more abstract understanding.

For example, in grades 2–5 the first chapter is about place value. The first lesson uses a concrete material such as base-ten materials or place-value chips to ensure that students can count, read, and write numbers. The second lesson introduces the place-value chart, which is used in every grade, as well as writing numbers in standard and expanded form. Students learn to compare numbers in the next lesson, and finally the last lesson focuses on finding place-value patterns.

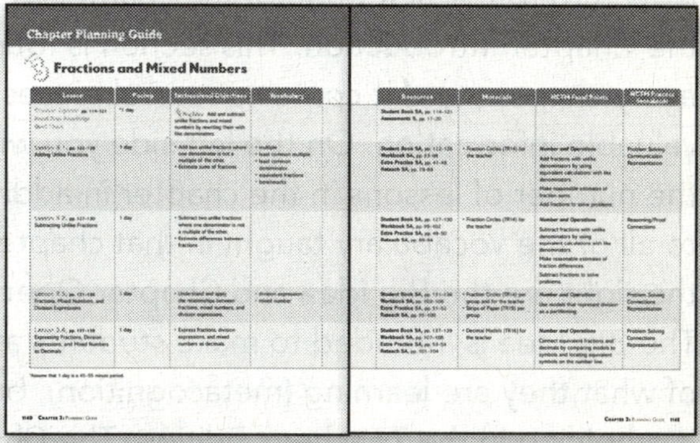

Grade 5 is shown as an example.

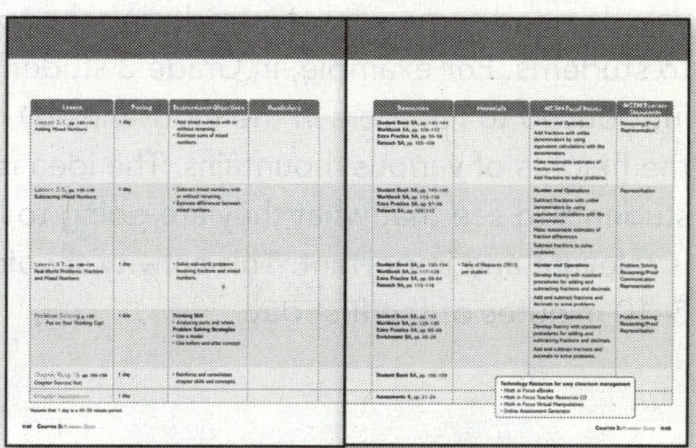

Grade 5 is shown as an example.

Chapter Introduction

Now turn to the first page of the chapter to see the Chapter Introduction. This section is found in every chapter, and it contains several pieces of valuable information. On the left side you will see the number of lessons in the chapter in addition to all of the vocabulary taught in that chapter. To the right are the Big Idea and Chapter Opener. The Big Idea is intended to make students aware of what they are learning (metacognition), but it is amplified in the Teacher's Edition. The Chapter Opener will help you introduce the new chapter to your students, providing context for the new topic. You may prefer to use a different context, but you do need some way of introducing the topic to students. For example, in Grade 3 students are introduced to numbers in the thousands by listing the heights of various mountains. The idea is for students to see that what they are going to learn is relevant and important. This activity should take 5–10 minutes of the first day.

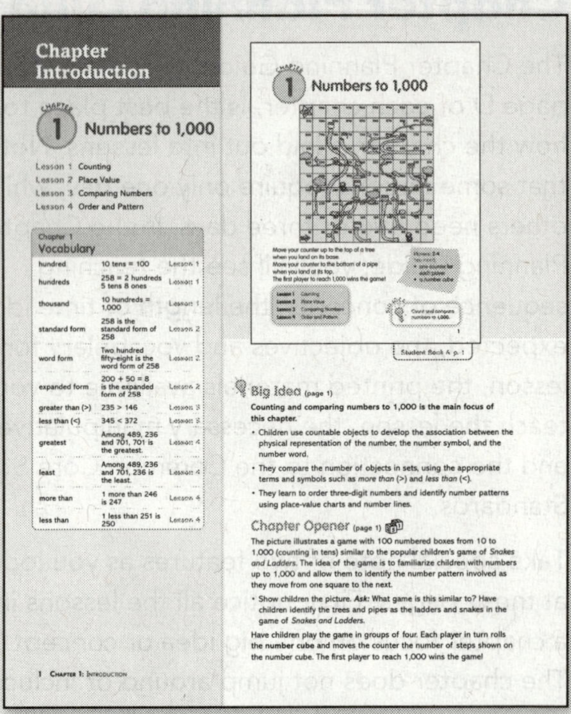

Grade 4 is shown as an example.

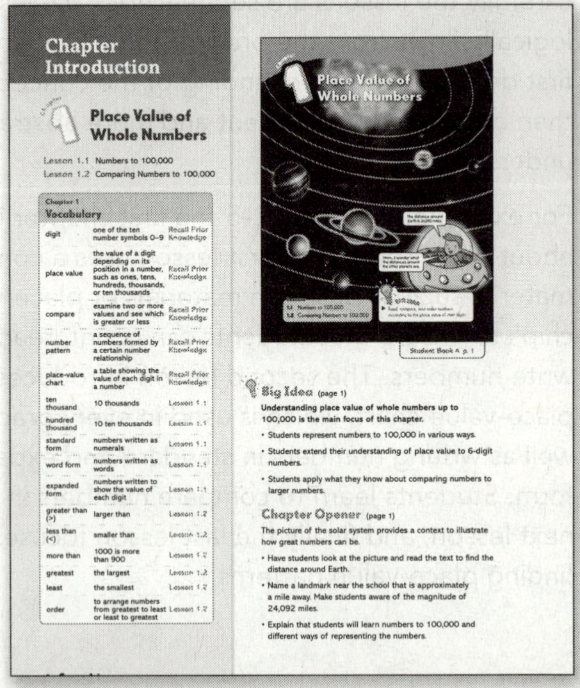

Grade 2 is shown as an example.

Recall Prior Knowledge and Quick Check

Before students begin a new chapter, you will need to ensure that they have the prerequisite knowledge to be successful in that chapter. To begin, use the Recall Prior Knowledge, found on the page after the Chapter Opener, to review material that was presented either in an earlier chapter or grade. Ask the questions provided to review the examples. By doing so, you are not giving them the information but rather checking how many students retained the information. It is natural for students to forget some of what they've learned, so this is an opportunity to stimulate them to remember. If some of the material is new, you will have to teach it now.

If students are struggling with the material, be sure to notice whether it is format, vocabulary, or content that causes the difficulty.

Finally on the first day, following the Chapter Opener and Recall Prior Knowledge, you will assign either the Quick Check or the pre-test from the Assessments book. The Quick Check is found in the Student Book, making it the more convenient choice, but the pre-test is a better test and is tied to the online Transition Resource Map.

The pre-test will tell you if students have the prior knowledge to be successful in the current chapter. If not, you will need the Transition Guide described on the next page. Be sure to see if there are patterns of errors in the pre-test because that can help you decide whether to include some additional support as you move into the chapter. For example, if a third grade student doesn't know "expanded form," he or she still could move into the chapter, but you would make a point of emphasizing this as you taught Chapter 1.

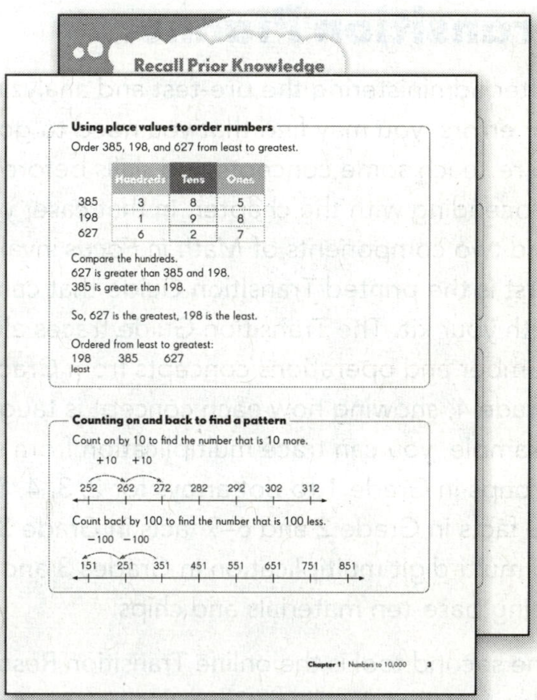

Grade 3 is shown as an example.

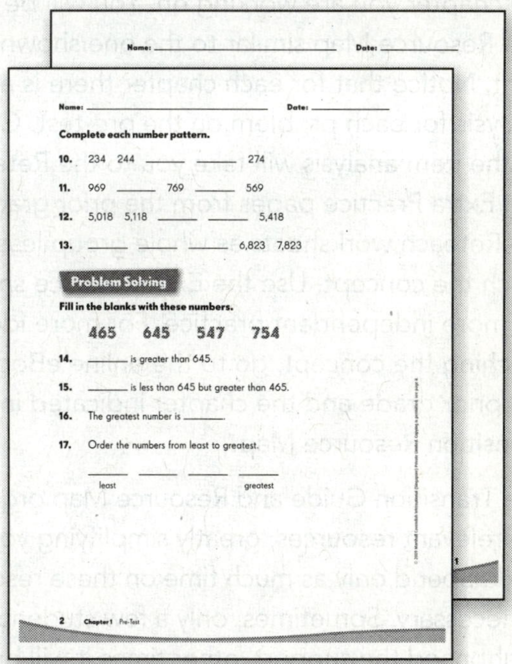

Grade 3 is shown as an example.

Transition Guide and Transition Planner

After administering the pre-test and analyzing it for errors, you may find that you need to go back to re-teach some concepts and skills before proceeding with the chapter. In that case, you will find two components of *Math in Focus* invaluable. First is the printed Transition Guide that came with your kit. The Transition Guide traces all the number and operations concepts from Grade 1 to Grade 4, showing how each concept is taught. For example, you can trace multiplication from simple groups in Grade 1 to dot arrays for 2, 3, 4, 5, and 10 facts in Grade 2 and 6–9 facts in Grade 3, then to multi-digit multiplication in Grades 3 and 4 using base-ten materials and chips.

The second tool is the online Transition Resource Map found at the Think Central Web site. As you find weaknesses in the pre-test, click on the Transition Resource Map for your grade, then select the chapter you are working on. You will be taken to a Resource Map similar to the one shown at the right. Notice that for each chapter there is an item analysis for each problem on the pre-test. Clicking on the item analysis will take you to the Reteach and Extra Practice pages from the prior grade. Use the Reteach worksheets as whole group lessons to teach the concept. Use the Extra Practice sheets for more independent practice. For more ideas on teaching the concept, go to the online eBook for the prior grade and the chapter indicated in the Transition Resource Map.

The Transition Guide and Resource Map organize the relevant resources, greatly simplifying your work. Spend only as much time on these resources as necessary. Sometimes, only a few students might need the support, other times it will be the whole class.

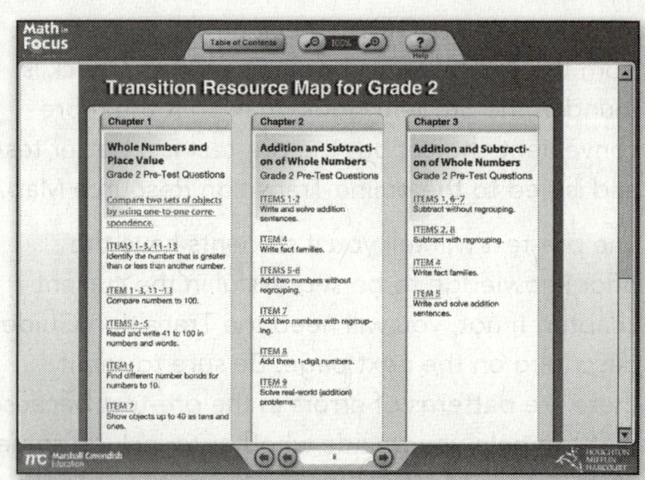

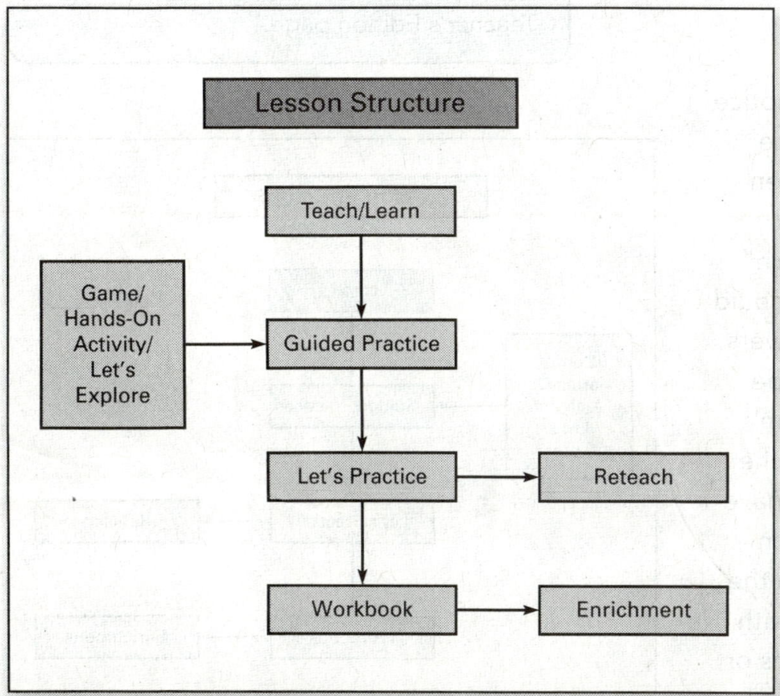

Lesson Structure for all *Math in Focus* Lessons

All *Math in Focus* lessons share the same structure, which is shown in the diagram above. Each part of the lesson will be discussed in more detail on the following pages.

Each lesson begins with a whole group lesson or mini-lesson called "Teach" in the Teacher's Edition and "Learn" in the Student Book. It is suggested that the student book should be closed during this portion.

Next comes the Guided Practice, or gradual release of responsibility to the student. This can be done with the whole group or with small groups by ability or to accommodate Response to Intervention (RtI). Students can also work with partners with teacher support.

Usually there is another Teach/Learn lesson and then another Guided Practice if the lesson has multiple objectives.

The Games, Let's Explore, and Hands-On Activities can be used in conjunction with Guided Practice to allow you to differentiate instruction and work in small groups.

Let's Practice is the independent practice done in the classroom that allows you to see whether students are ready to work independently in the Workbook. It is formative assessment and should be used to guide remediation or additional instruction.

If students are unsuccessful in Let's Practice, they will need to use the Reteach materials. If successful in Let's Practice, students are ready for the Workbook. Students can do one page in class and one or two pages at home for homework depending on the length of your math period.

If the homework pages are too easy, the students can be assigned pages from the Enrichment book. These are challenging problems on the same topic.

Lesson Planning

Teach/Learn

Now you are ready to teach the lessons. Notice that the first page of the lesson includes the necessary vocabulary and materials and then describes a whole group lesson. It is called "Teach" in the Teacher's Edition and "Learn" In the Student Book. The Student Books should be closed at this point because all the answers are on the page. Teach/Learn is meant to be an active component. The Teacher's Edition gives instructions on what to do and what the dialogue might look like. Students should have manipulatives—interlocking cubes, base-ten materials, fraction strips, etc.—as shown in the picture for the lesson. Students can work with partners or individually as you ask questions or model the concept. You will need to decide how to display what is shown on the page. Some possibilities are to place the manipulatives on a rug or to display them on an overhead, document camera, or interactive whiteboard. Finally, think of the questions you will ask as you teach the lesson.

For example, in the lesson to the right from Chapter 1 in Grade 3, students are learning to read, write and understand numbers to 1,000. The student book should be closed as you direct the students to display 4 hundreds, 2 tens, and 5 ones, asking what number is represented. You ask the students how they know it is 425. Working with a partner, students next stack ten hundreds and count by hundreds, ending with one thousand. You can then ask how many hundreds make a thousand and write the answer on the board. Students might record something similar in a math journal. If necessary, you might repeat these activities with other numbers.

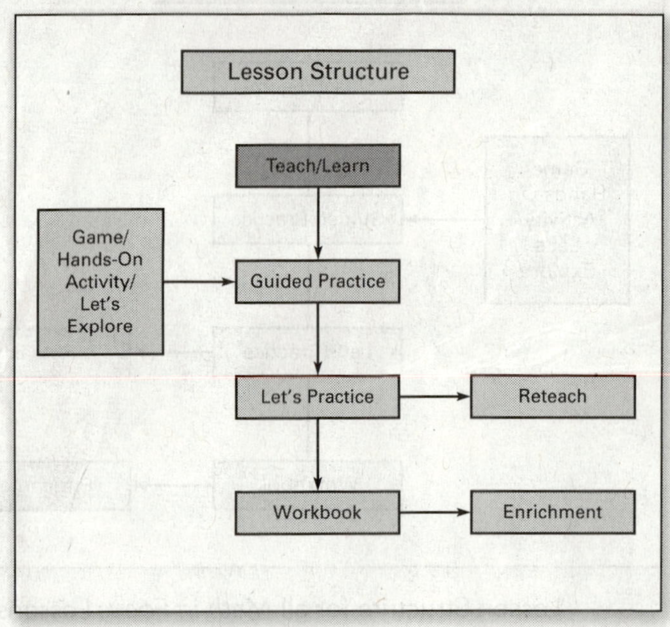

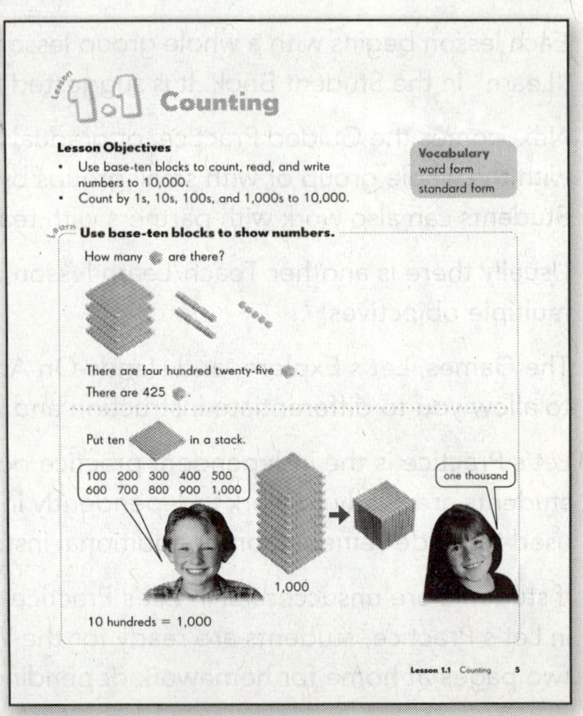

Grade 3 is shown as an example.

Guided Practice

Immediately after the Teach/Learn lesson, you will see something called Guided Practice. Guided Practice is intended to provide practice for the students, but with teacher support. At first, this activity might be done with the whole class. The difference between Guided Practice and the Teach/Learn lesson is that you will ask questions more than model. You support the first few problems but then gradually release responsibility so students are trying them on their own. Guided Practice provides more examples for practice and indicates to you if your students are ready to work independently.

The Guided Practice contains problems similar to the Teach/Learn examples. You may see pictures of manipulatives in these problems. You will need to decide if students are ready for the pictorial representation or if they need to get out the materials. Sometimes the Guided Practice will be at the abstract level, and again you will need to assess whether students can work at that level or need a picture or concrete material.

In the example to the right, students are practicing writing standard and word form for numbers to 10,000 in Grade 3. Notice the first few problems include visual models, which students should be able to interpret. The rest of the problems are more abstract, asking students to convert from word form to standard form and vice versa. The idea is to help them with the first problems, but then see if students can do the rest of each set on their own. If they can, then you know that they understand the concept.

You may find that you can have some students work in pairs on the Guided Practice while you work with the remaining students.

Finally, notice that often there is another Teach/Learn lesson and Guided Practice that follows.

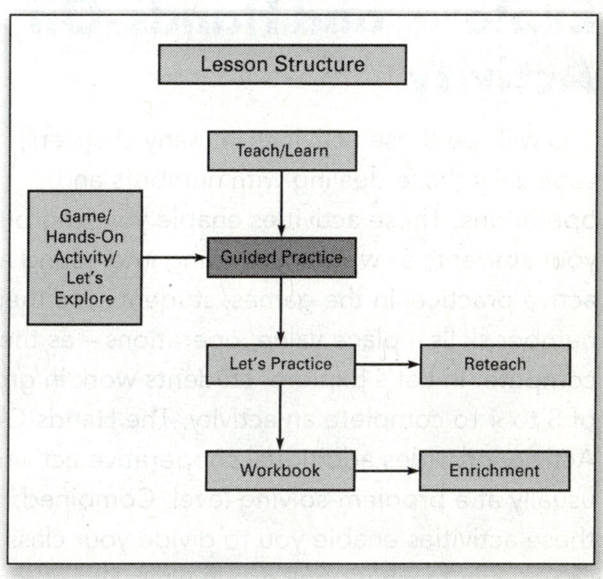

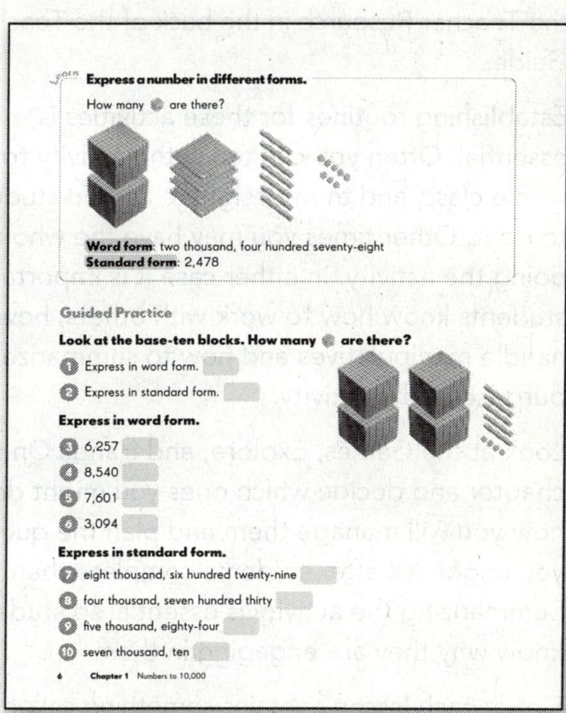

Grade 3 is shown as an example.

Activities: Games, Let's Explore, and Hands-On Activity

You will see these activities in many chapters, especially those dealing with numbers and operations. These activities enable you to group your students as well as providing interesting and active practice. In the games, students use their number skills – place value, operations – as they compete. In Let's Explore, students work in groups of 3 to 4 to complete an activity. The Hands-On Activity provides additional cooperative activities, usually at a problem-solving level. Combined, these activities enable you to divide your class so you can teach a small group while the other students are doing the activity.

In general you will find that the games and activities do not involve many parts or pieces. When a board or number cards are necessary, they are available in the Teacher Resource in the back of the Teacher's Guide.

Establishing routines for these activities is essential. Often you can teach the activity to the whole class, and then designate certain students to do it. Other times you may have the whole class doing the activity. In either case it is important that students know how to work with others, how to handle manipulatives and how to summarize the purpose of the activity.

Look at the Games, Explore, and Hands On in the chapter and decide which ones you might do. Plan how you will manage them and plan the questions you might ask after students complete them. Summarizing the activity is essential so students know why they are engaging in them.

Finally each lesson contains something called Problem of the Lesson. You can use these as warmups or exit tickets after you have taught the lesson.

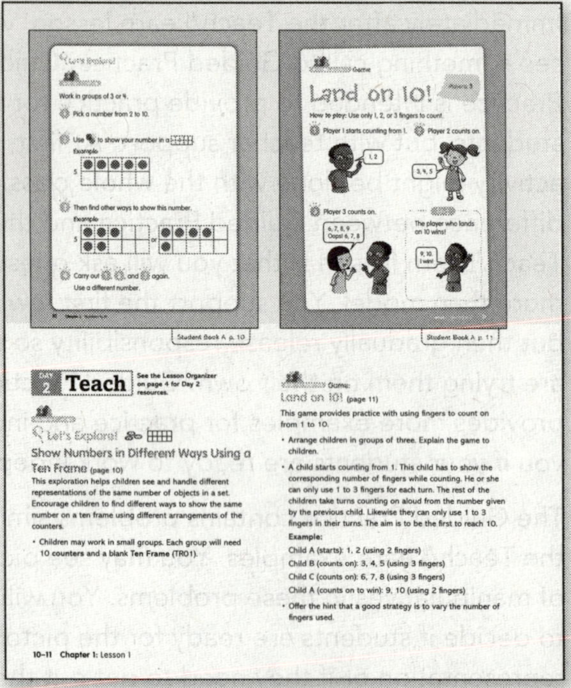

Grade 1 is shown as an example.

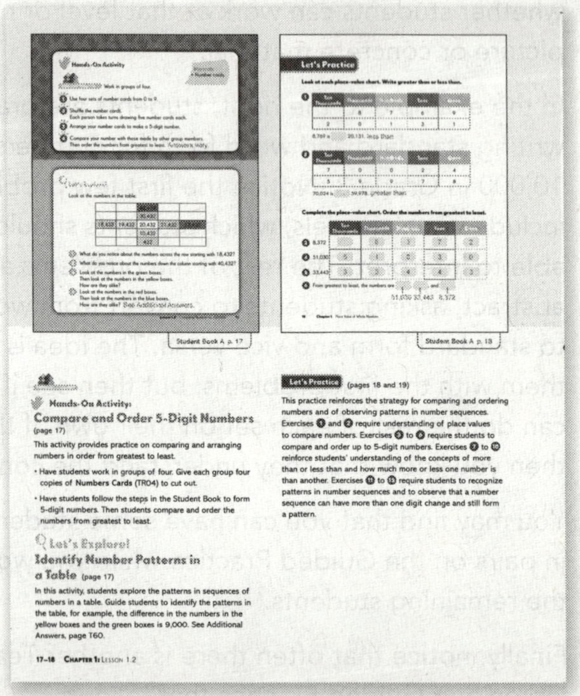

Grade 4 is shown as an example.

Let's Practice: Independent Practice

After several rounds of whole group and guided practice, you should see the feature called Let's Practice. It will appear at the end of the lesson in either a one-day or multiple day lesson. Let's Practice is intended as formative assessment for you to decide if students are ready to work independently in the workbook. Students will need their books to do these. They number their paper or notebook and work independently on completing all of the problems. Notice that some problems contain visual models and others are abstract. The problems also increase in complexity. One problem may simply ask students what number has 3 tens and 5 ones and a couple of problems later it may ask "30 is __ tens and 10 ones" to see if students have really mastered the concept of ones and tens in first grade.

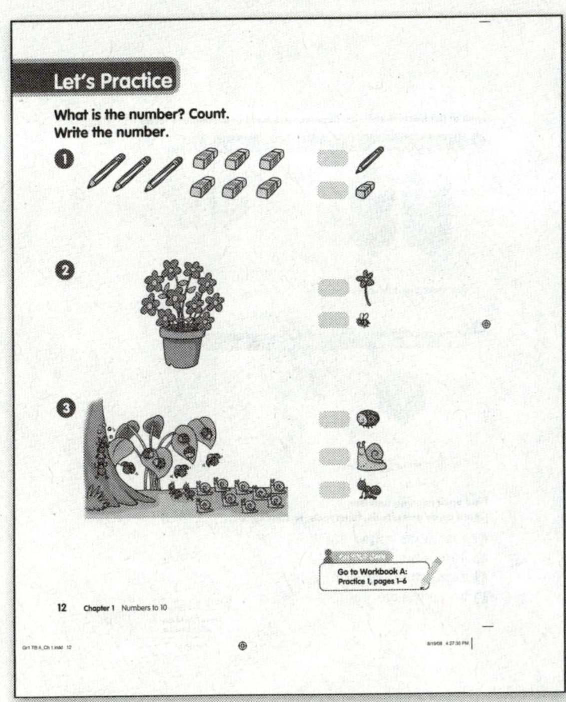

Grade 1 is shown as an example.

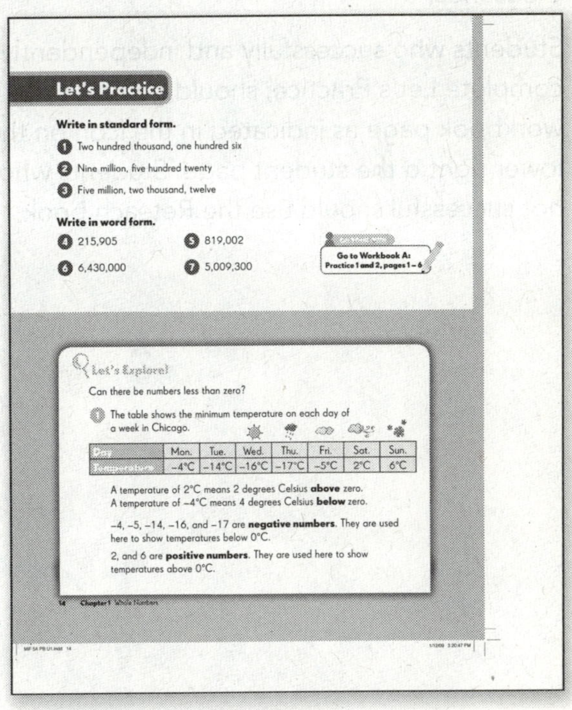

Grade 5 is shown as an example.

In the primary grades you can use individual white boards as well as notebooks or other paper. Students can't write in their books, so the first few times you will have to model how to number and record answers. Dividing a small white board into 4 quadrants and numbering it 1-4 on the front and 5-8 on the back is helpful.

In all the grades, be sure to circulate. If students are struggling, you can stop this activity or limit the ones the student needs to do. Remember, the purpose for this activity is for you to get a good sense of how many students are ready to work independently and on what topics. Look for patterns of errors to know what to re-teach.

In the sample from 3rd grade, students first must be able to understand pictorial models of numbers in the thousands, then use their knowledge of place value to determine the numbers in a pattern based on increasing either ones, tens, hundreds or thousands.

Students who successfully and independently complete Let's Practice, should go on to the workbook page as indicated in the icon on the lower right o the student page. Students who are not successful should use the Reteach book.

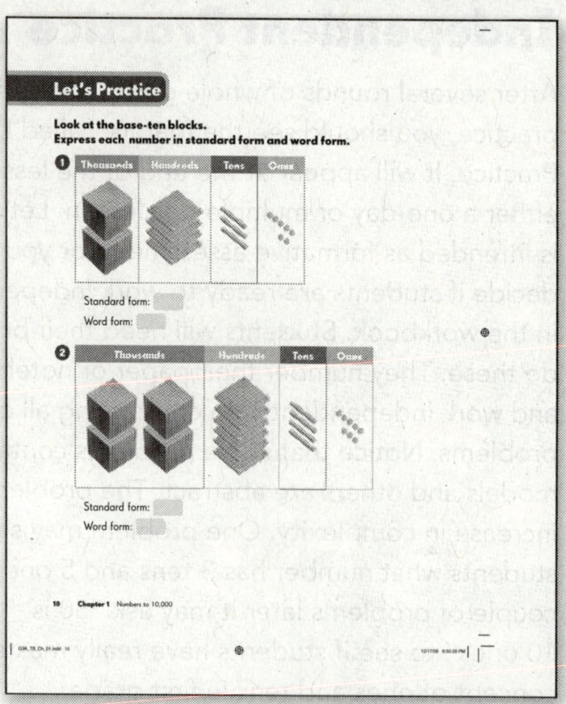

Grade 3 is shown as an example.

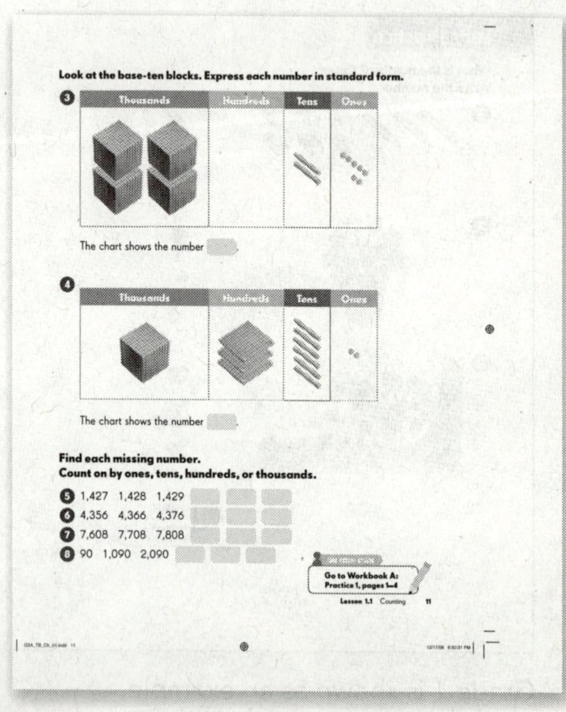

Grade 3 is shown as an example.

Workbook: Independent Practice

Look for the workbook pages at the end of Lesson 1. You should see 4 or more sheets. These worksheets are intended to be done both in class as independent practice and as homework pages. Usually you will assign one in class and one or two to take home. Students should NOT be doing the workbook pages until they can successfully do them. The purpose of these pages is to practice and become fluent, not to learn. That is why they are assigned only after the student demonstrates competence in the Let's Practice.

The workbook pages parallel the work done in Teach/Learn and Guided Practice. Most pages begin with examples that use pictorial models, then include more abstract questions. Primary grades have lots of pictorial models so there is a minimum of reading. Students should be familiar with the questions, but you may have to go over them before sending them home. Check for understanding before they take them home.

You will also notice there are sometimes as many as 5 or 6 worksheets. That is because the next lessons are usually multiple day lessons and there won't be independent practice for the first day. You can use the workbook pages from the previous lesson so students continue to practice at home.

The key to the workbook pages is to make sure students are able to do them before assigning them. If students are struggling you may need to give them the Reteach or Extra Practice worksheets. Notice how the first grade sheets above include an example so parents will understand what is being asked of the student.

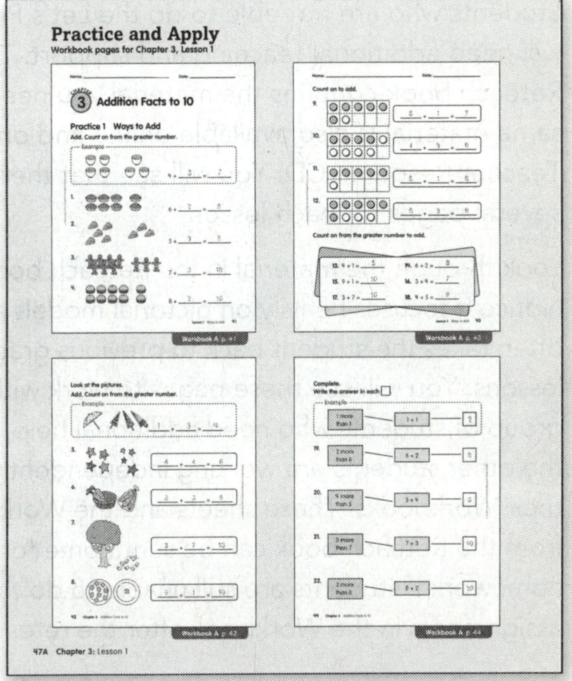

Grade 1 is shown as an example.

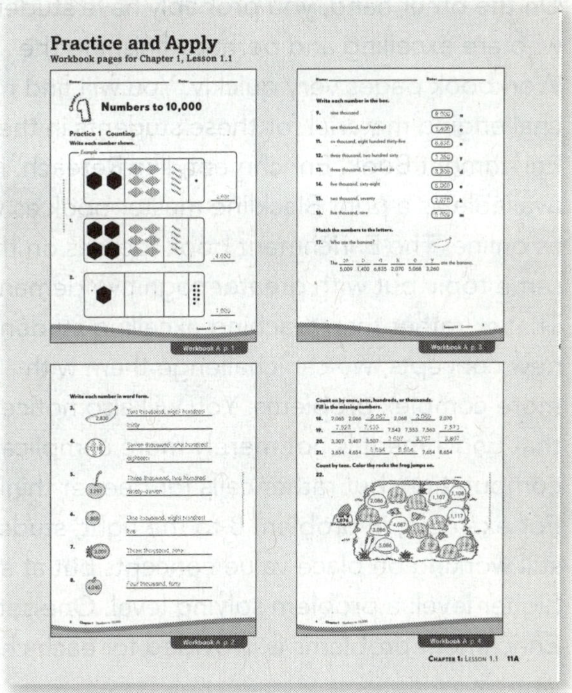

Grade 3 is shown as an example.

Reteach

Students who are not able to do the Let's Practice will need additional teaching and support. The Reteach book contains the material you need. The same material is also available online and on the Teacher Resource CD. You will see that there are several pages for each lesson.

Look through the material in the Reteach book. Notice it focuses heavily on pictorial models and often takes the student back to previous grades or lessons. You will use these pages to work with the group of students who need additional help, while the other students are working independently in their Workbooks. These sheets and the Worksheets from the Reteach book can be sent home for homework if students are still unable to do the assignments in the Workbook after the reteaching.

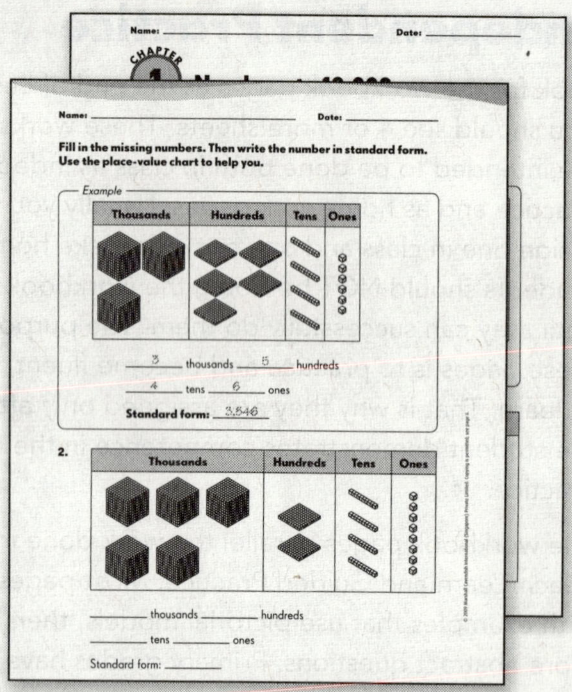

Grade 3 is shown as an example.

Enrichment

On the other hand, you probably have students who are excelling and perhaps finishing the Workbook pages very quickly. You will find more challenging material for these students in the Enrichment Book. Enrichment, like Reteach, is available as a print Blackline master book as well as online. The Enrichment book focuses on the same topic but with greater cognitive demands. That is, rather than teaching excelling students new concepts, we can challenge them with more complex problems. You will also notice that Enrichment is not merely more complicated computation, but rather calls for deeper thinking. For example, in problem 8 to the right, students are still working on place value concepts but at a much higher level: a problem solving level. One set of Enrichment problems is provided for each chapter.

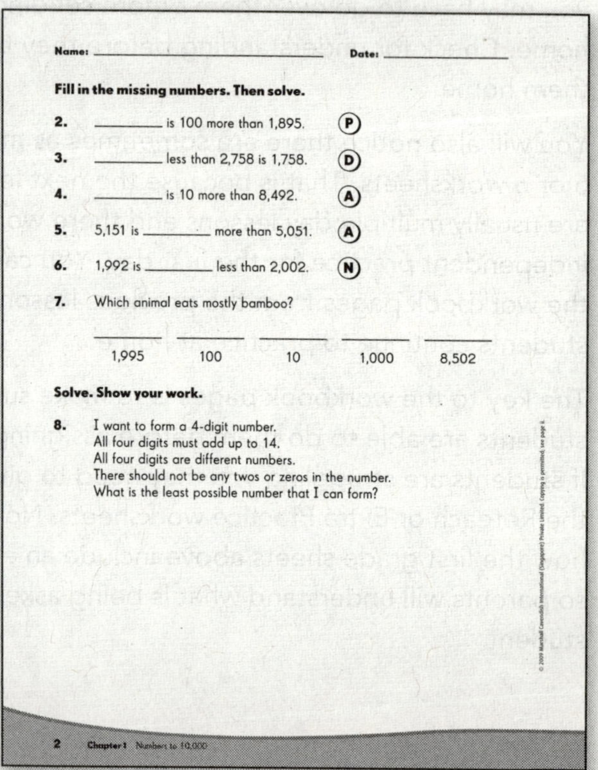

Grade 3 is shown as an example.

Additional Chapter Features

Put on Your Thinking Cap! and Math Journal

Besides solving, students also need repeated opportunities to solve non-routine problems, which require students to synthesize the concepts, skills, and strategies they have acquired. This type of problem, labeled Put on Your Thinking Cap! is found at the end of every chapter. Students can work on these problems independently or in small groups. Your role is to encourage persistence, to ask guiding questions, and to help students summarize solutions and strategies. Several different problem solving strategies are suggested in the Teacher's Edition; use these as needed to guide students to think about which strategy works best for them in this situation. The Workbook contains two or three additional Put on Your Thinking Cap! problems that can be done in class and as homework.

As you begin, think of questions to help students get started without revealing the whole answer. After students have completed the problems, summarize the solutions so students can apply them in the Workbook problems. If students work in groups of two or four, model how students should work together. Remember, the focus of these problems is the thinking necessary to solve them, not just the solutions.

The Math Journal encourages students to explain their thinking through writing and to see that math is about thinking and reasoning. Often the Math Journal will model what a good answer might look like. Be sure to review this model with your students.

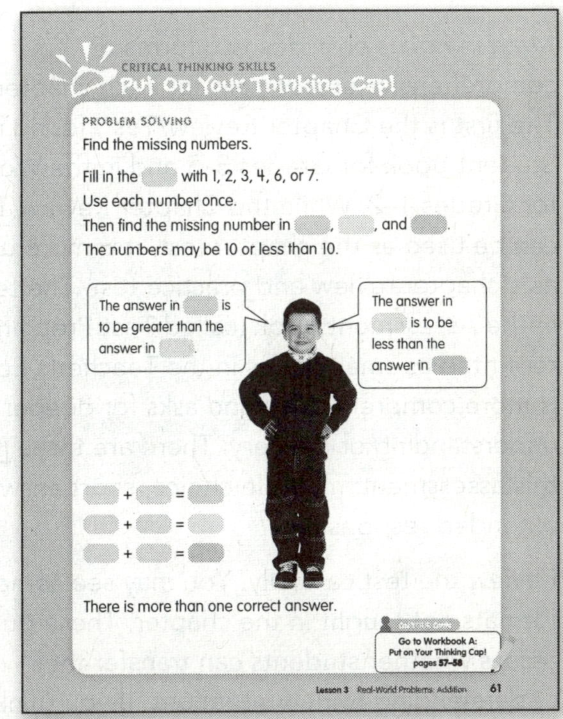

Grade 1 is shown as an example.

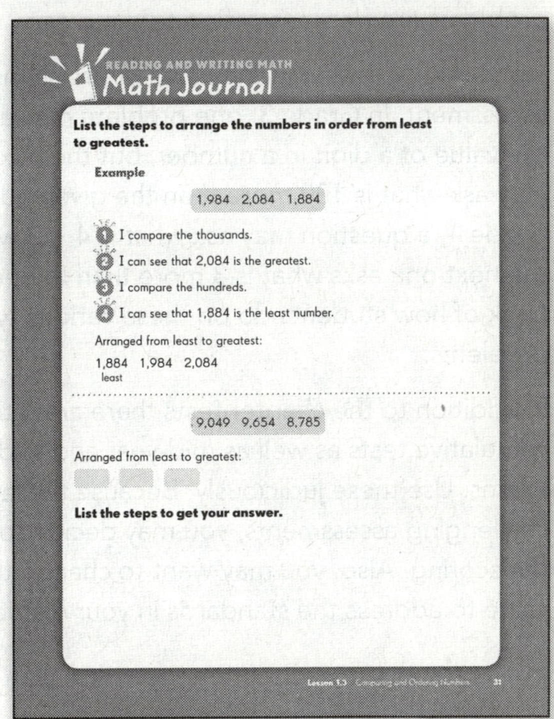

Grade 3 is shown as an example.

Assessment

Math in Focus provides two forms of comprehensive assessment for each chapter. The first is the Chapter Review/Test, found in the Student Book for Grades 3–5 and in the Workbook for Grades 1–2. While the Chapter Review/Test can be used as the chapter test, it is more useful as a chapter review and practice test. The test in the Assessment book (called Test Prep and reprinted as small pages in the Teacher's Edition) is more comprehensive and asks for deeper understanding or mastery. There are three parts to this assessment: multiple choice, short answer, and extended response.

Review the test carefully. You may see some formats not taught in the chapter. These questions assess whether students can transfer their understanding to new situations. If you think some of these questions are too difficult, give them as extra credit questions. Students who can do these problems are demonstrating true mastery.

Notice the variation in the kinds of problems in the assessment. In Grade 3, one problem may ask for the value of a digit in a number, but the next item may ask what is 100 more than the given number. In Grade 1, a question may ask what is 4 + 3 while the next one asks what is 3 more than 5. Keeping track of how students do on these various types of problems.

In addition to the chapter tests there are 6 to 8 cumulative tests as well as mid-year and end-of-year exams. Use these judiciously. Because these are challenging assessments, you may decide to adjust the scoring. Also, you may want to change the point value to address the standards in your district.

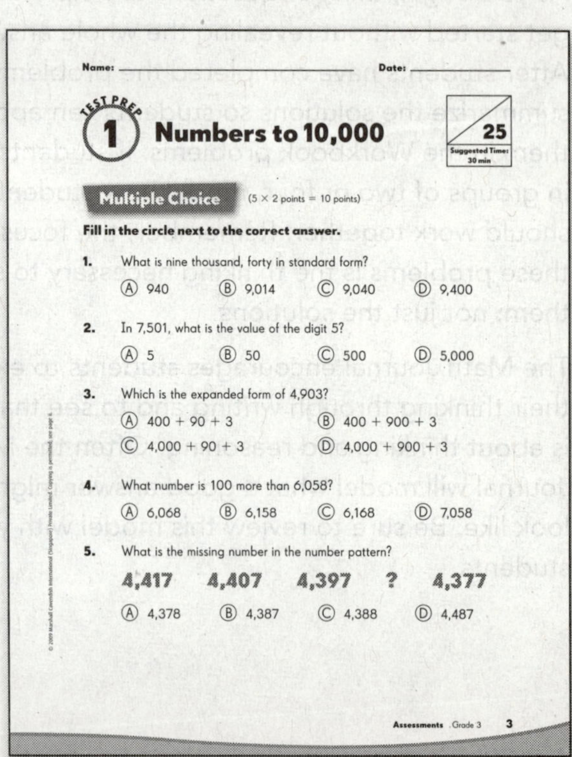

Grade 3 is shown as an example.

Concrete to Pictorial to Abstract Pedagogy

At the heart of *Math In Focus* is the remarkably effective pedagogy of starting from concrete materials, then connecting these materials to pictorial representations, and finally visualizing those representations when solving problems abstractly. The goal is to develop abstract understanding. This sequence is not linear but moves fluidly back and forth, providing enough concrete experiences to develop conceptual understanding, and enough visual models to enable abstract fluency. Much of this pedagogy stems from the work of Jerome Bruner, whom the Singapore Math authors cite often. Bruner explained that students could do very abstract reasoning and even problem solving if they had a material to act it out with. He also explained the importance of visualization in developing understanding.

Let's look at some examples. In Grade 1, students use number bonds and ten frames to develop an understanding of adding and subtracting quantities to 20. The number bond is a visual model for showing part-part-whole relationships. Students begin with interlocking cubes and divide them into two quantities. They put the cubes into the number bond framework and then assign numbers for the parts and the whole. Eventually, we want students to be able to visualize these number bonds when performing simple operations. Similarly, the ten frames are used to organize quantities so they are easily recognizable without counting. Students learn to build 5 on top, some on the bottom, and memorize the number of empty spaces. In that way, when they are adding numbers whose sum is greater than 10, they can always fill in the first number to ten, and then add the rest. In other words, $8 + 4 = 8 + 2 + 2$. If done abstractly, some students might not understand this, but when done with cubes and ten frames it becomes accessible to all students.

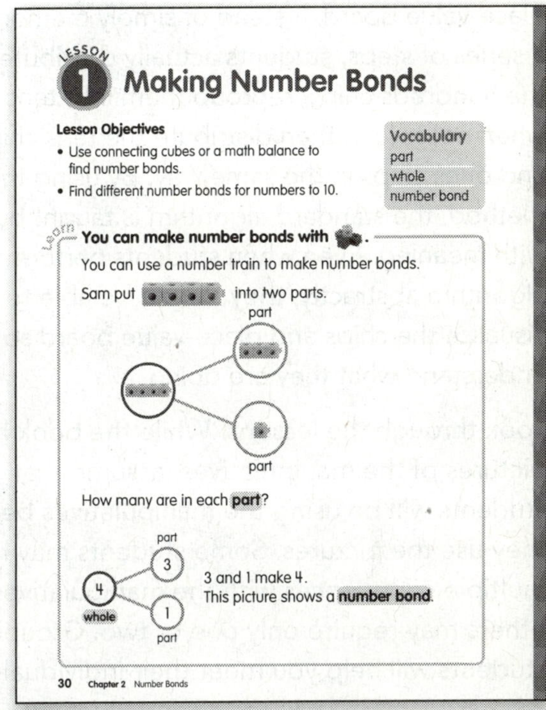

Grade 1 is shown as an example.

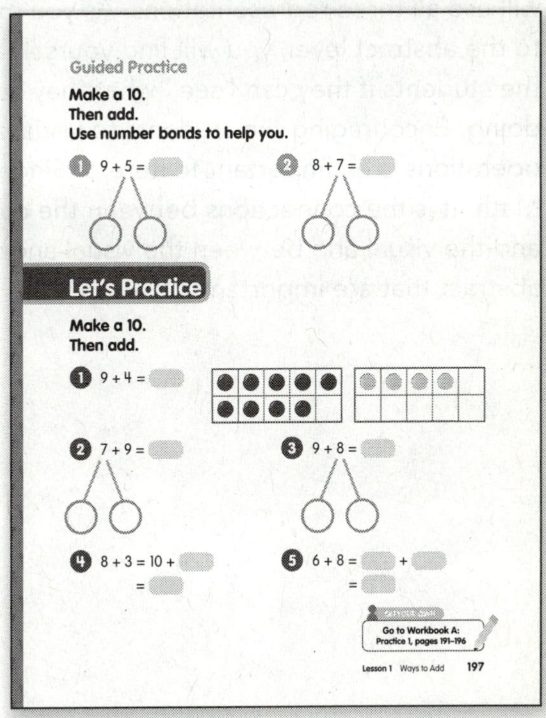

Grade 1 is shown as an example.

In Grade 4, students learn the long division algorithm by using place-value chips on a place-value board. Instead of simply memorizing a series of steps, students actually distribute the hundreds chips, regroup them into tens when necessary, then distribute the tens chips and ones chips in the same way. By using this method, the standard algorithm is taught but with meaning. Even when students perform the algorithm abstractly, they should be able to visualize the chips and place-value board so they understand what they are doing.

Look through the lessons. While the book has pictures of the manipulatives, assume that students will be using the manipulatives before they use the pictures. Some students may require multiple experiences with the manipulatives, while others may require only one or two. Grouping students will help you meet their individual needs.

This sequence—concrete to pictorial to abstract—is used throughout *Math in Focus*. Most days you will use all three representations. As you move to the abstract level, you will find yourself asking the students if they can "see" what they are doing. Encouraging the students to visualize the operations is an important feature of Singapore Math. It is the connections between the concrete and the visual and between the visual and the abstract that are important.

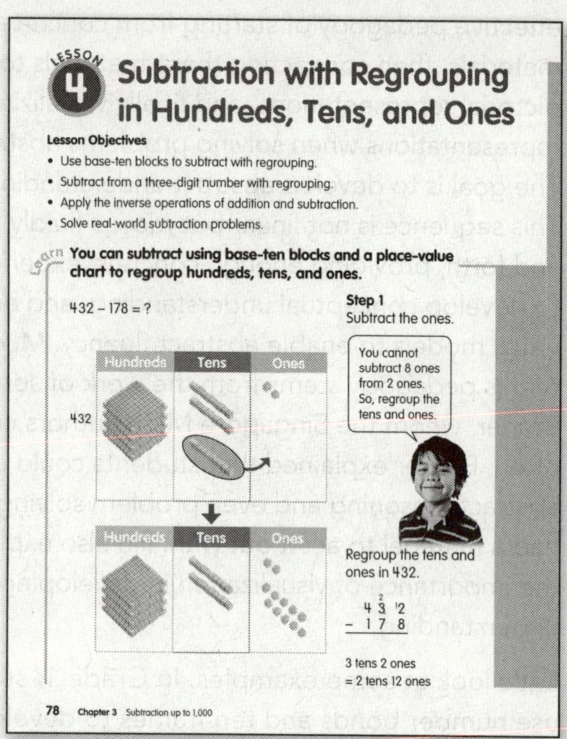

Grade 2 is shown as an example.

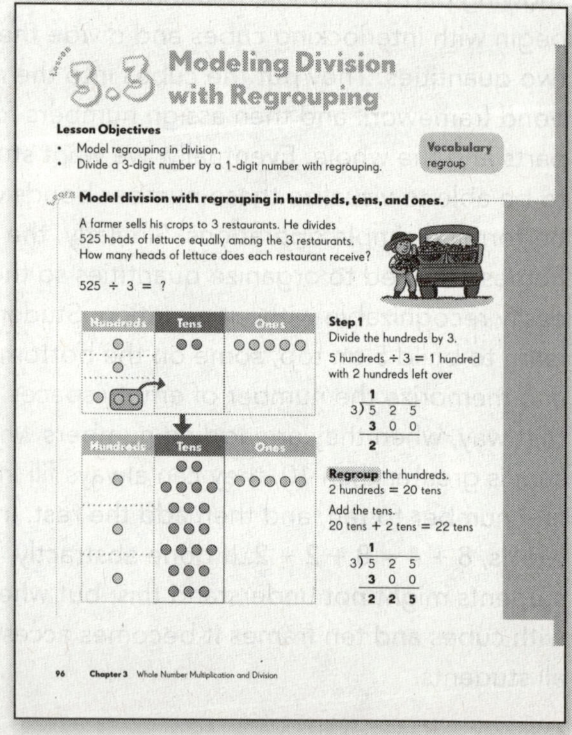

Grade 4 is shown as an example.

Technology Resources

Teacher Tip:

To learn more about *Math In Focus*, be sure to visit the eLearning Web site: hmhelearning.com. Online program resources are on http://www.k6.thinkcentral.com.

By now you realize that you have a wealth of resources to teach all the students in your classroom. But increasingly, classrooms are also introducing new technology. *Math in Focus* includes a variety of technology resources to enhance the learning experience.

First, all of the printed material is available online. eBook format:

- Student Book
- Teacher's Edition

Printable PDF format:

- Reteach
- Enrichment
- Extra Practice
- Assessments
- School-to-Home Connections

An Online Assessment Generator, Lesson Planner, and Online Transition Resources are also available. Each teacher and student will receive his or her own log-in information, so you can plan from home without having to bring the books home each day.

In addition, there is a set of virtual manipulatives that include base-ten materials, place-value chips, counters and interlocking cubes, number lines, balances, clocks, geometric shapes, function machines, bar models and number bonds, money and many more. While none of these can substitute for the actual objects, once the objects have been introduced in the class, you can use these to extend many of the activities. If you are fortunate enough to have an interactive whiteboard, you can use these virtual manipulatives on them for interactive activities. There are also interactive whiteboard lessons available for each lesson in *Math in Focus*.

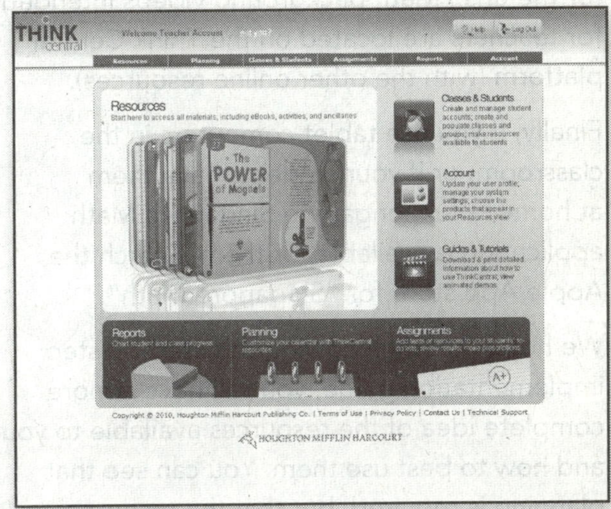

Teacher Tip:

If you have additional questions, visit the *Math in Focus* eLearning Web site at hmhelearning.com or our Web site at www.hmheducation.com/mathinfocus.

Additionally, videos and podcasts are available for teachers and parents to explain what we are teaching and why. When parents and teachers work together, students benefit enormously. These are located on our eLearning site and our Web site. (See Teacher Tip on next page for the urls.) Math Background videos intended for teachers are located on the Think Central platform (with the other online resources).

Finally, if you use tablet computers in the classroom, or if your students have them at home, a fun, engaging Singapore Math application is available for them. Search the Apple App store for "Singapore Math".

We hope that by following this step-by-step implementation guide, you will have a more complete idea of the resources available to you and how to best use them. You can see that planning is required, but that the resources you need to effectively teach all students are available.

Some of the practices that have proven helpful as teachers begin this program include:

- Work with your fellow teachers to plan a chapter at a time, rather than a day or even week at a time.

- Write as many questions as you can into the Teacher's Edition so you are ready with appropriate questions when you are teaching.

- Recognize that the first year, some of this approach will be new to you and your students and may require more time than is suggested in the Teacher's Edition.

- Study the assessments carefully both before and after students take them, first to understand the goal, and second to analyze patterns of errors.

- Use the concrete to pictorial to abstract approach in daily lessons.

- Recognize the subtle differences as each lesson builds on the previous one, adding a new level of understanding.

- Teach for mastery.

- Most of all, enjoy the satisfaction you will feel when students say math is their favorite subject and they love solving problems.

- Finally, please join our online community on Facebook **www.facebook.com/mathinfocus**, Twitter, and our blog **www.singaporemathblog.com** to share with other educators using *Math in Focus*.

<u>Non-Negotiables of Math in Focus</u>

1. Concrete ➤ Pictorial ➤ Abstract (CPA)
    ↳ manipulatives

2. Visualization
    ↳ in your minds eye
    ↳ manipulate numbers in their mind

3. Math is thinking.
    ↳ questioning, discovery

4. Gradual Release

Books closed during discussion/
    teach/learn time

Ch. Test in Book - Review
Test Prep - actual assessment

Do pre-test
    (skip quick check if needed)

part × part = whole

whole ÷ part = part

make poster

→ Teach/Learn Box → take it off the page!!!
(anchor tasks)

→ guided Learning
(partners)

<u>Let's practice</u>
- games
- hands on
- let's explore
- guided learning

partners
groups

workbook pages - independent

Look at assessment when planning chapter.

Day to Day plans - gradual release

Dr. Yeap Ban

<u>Planning</u>

What is the intent?

- How will content be presented?
- How will I break it down?
- How will I build it up?
- How will students engage in the lesson?

Anchor Tasks - exploring (main learning task
core concept

(first lesson, first teach/learn box)

group discovery
    questions that can't be answered
    with yes/no
strategies explained by students

anchor task becomes anchor chart
    (their thinking becomes anchor charts)

(Learning objective in bold)

• Less is more

• Think about multiple
    strategies

• Have a key question!

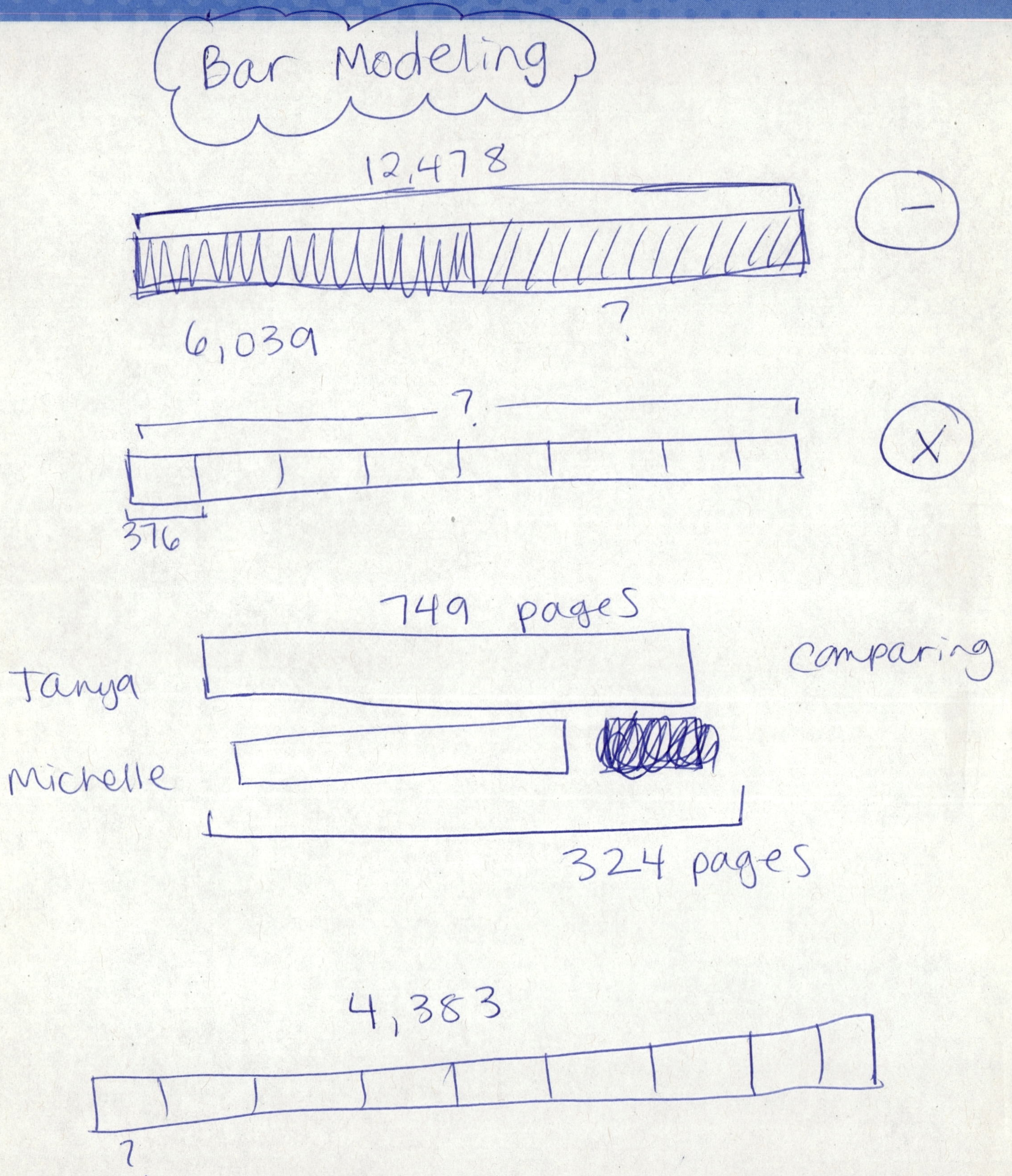

Bar Modeling
12,478
6,039
?
—
?
×
376
749 pages
Tanya
Michelle
comparing
324 pages
4,383
?